Don't Call Me Nigger

Don't Call Me Nigger

By:

Marjorie Y. Booker

ISBN 1-58500-183-X

ABOUT THE BOOK

Prejudice prevents us from developing because we block our minds with preconceived negativism. Prejudice is a cancerous sore that disguises itself in belittling and insulting language. This type of speech creates an unintelligent and deceptive wall between individuals or people who have felt the pain of racism. Thus it is hoped that a better understanding and respect can be achieved. Our pluralistic society demands that we respect each other, if we're to survive and ultimately live together. It's time that we talk rather than fight; respect rather than hate.

DEDICATION

This booklet is dedicated in honor of my beloved Mother, the late Mother Mary Evadney McLachlan who worked with our late father, Bishop L. O. McLachlan - the first Bishop of the Church of God in Christ in England, Ireland, Scotland and Wales. I also dedicate this book to my dear family.

TABLE OF CONTENTS

DON'T CALL ME NIGGER

Don't call me nigger!
You don't know me.
Whether I come from
The Black land of Africa
From the islands of the Seas
Or the other lands of this universe,
I'm not to be judged by
The pigmentation of my skin
Or by the texture of my hair.
Who are you to judge me
Anyway?
Don't call me nigger!
You don't know me.
You don't know my family heritage
You definitely do not know
The heritage of my race.
Look at the civilization of Africa
And you'll learn from whence
I came.
I'm proud to be black - hope
You can say the same for your race.
I've ran with kings and queens
Blessed the lands with the
Toil of my sweat
And the shedding of my blood.
Don't call me nigger!
You don't know me.
I've toiled and worked; I've contributed

1

Not only to my race, but to humanity -
White, yellow, red, brown and black;
They've all learned from me.
Out into this darkened world
They've gone to redeem humanity
From the wisdom, knowledge and love of my store.
The world shall be a better place
Because I have come to earth -
Can you say that about you?
Don't call me nigger!
You don't know me.
Just keep stepping, if you will
I'll be me and better still.
If you looked deep inside of me
Then and only then, you'll know me.

DON'T CALL ME A NAME

Don't call me a name
I do not know;
Then stand back
Like a man with intelligence.
Scrutinize my work
Observe my strides
Investigate my resume
Then you'll never assume
I'm nobody because I'm black.
Do you really believe you're
Somebody just because you're white?
No! You don't really think so
And I'm not that dumb
Though some of us look like a bum.
A person's worth is not on the
Outside of his flesh
It's in the heart, deep inside
Where your eye can't penetrate.
So stop being so hostile and irate;
Use your head to think and heart to perceive.
A person's worth is not in
The color that painted his skin,
But is calculated by the quality of his being.

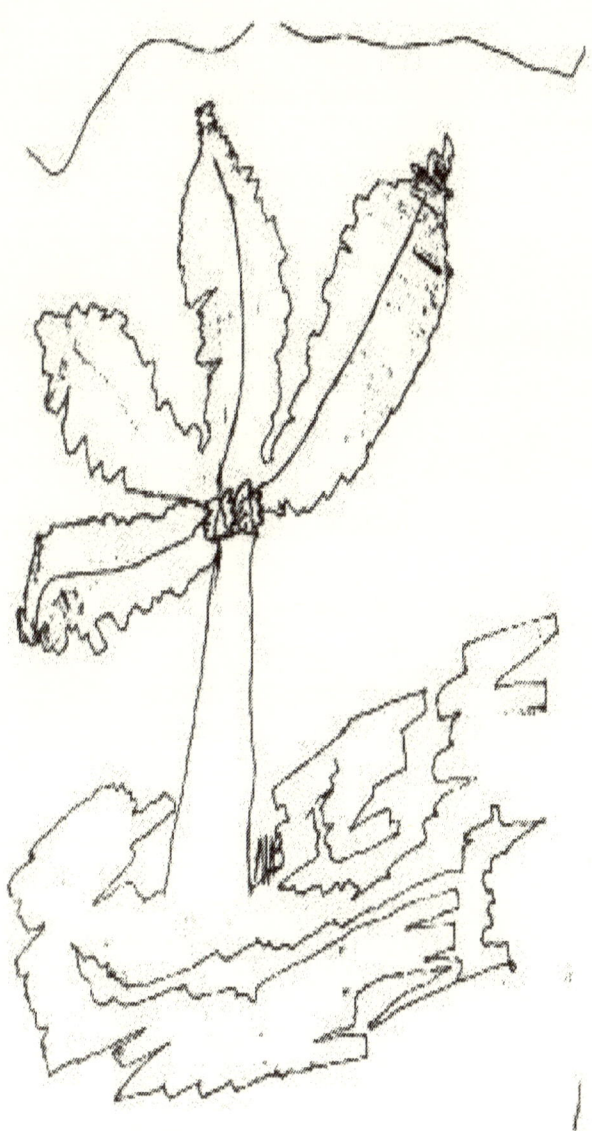

AFFIRMATIVE ACTION

Affirmative Action
Down the drain
Like heavy rains
Washing the streets clean.
But are we really
Ready to go out into
The world
And treat every man
The way he should be treated?
I hope so; then
Affirmative Action-
Building beautiful blocks
To equality and justice
Will not be needed
Because we're all
Given the same fair chance.
Naturally, that's all we ask.
We don't have to beg
For the crumbs falling
From any man's table.
Just let justice
And freedom prevail
And we shall all march to victory.

LAWLESS LAW

Can we legislate the heart
That is so unpredictable, vile and wicked?
Can we ask each other to be just
When to outrun others is a must?
Who makes laws to protect us all?
Who fights to see that justice prevails?
Who covers me to discover the truth?
Whether black or white, rich or poor?
Justice shall only prevail when we
Recognize the justice of God
For whether we honor Him or not
Our judicial system was created
On the principles of Judo-Christian teachings.
Who shall see to it
That every one is justly treated?
Let's pray that people everywhere
Arise to the occasion
To bring this world to a sanity
It has never truly known.
Hypocrisy, murder, killing, stealing
Have plagued our world too long.
Human hearts humiliated with shame
Rock the universe in bitter slavery-
A slavery with chain, sweat and tears
Because Injustice is the worst slavery,
And we shall all have to pay
Sooner or later, sooner or later.
Pay day is coming! Pay day is coming!

Sooner or later, sooner or later.

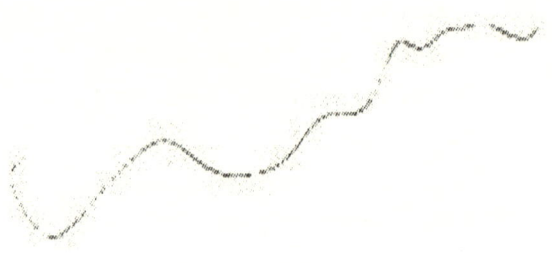

IRONIC IMAGE

Nigger is a bad word
Don't let it come out
of thy sacred mouth
Aren't you too undefiled
Like the pure lily

To say ugly, nasty, disgusting words?
Don't use words that would
Defile thy hypocritical purity.
Say words that are kind
Words to demonstrate intelligence.
Nigger is a bad word
Let's make it a crime.
We justly talk about pornography
Violence, vulgarity and immorality
But don't we know that
"Nigger" is a bad word?
It is a crime to use that word
It's violence, vulgarity and immorality
To use the word "nigger."
Don't use that word, please don't!
Don't use a word so cold
Like freezing, futile filth.
Let that word, "nigger" die
Let it die, Let it die.
That word brings memories
I want to eradicate.
That word chills dreams
I want to create.
Let the word "nigger" die
Let it die, Let it die!
Or someone may have to cry
Cry, Cry, Cry.
Don't ask me why I know, why.

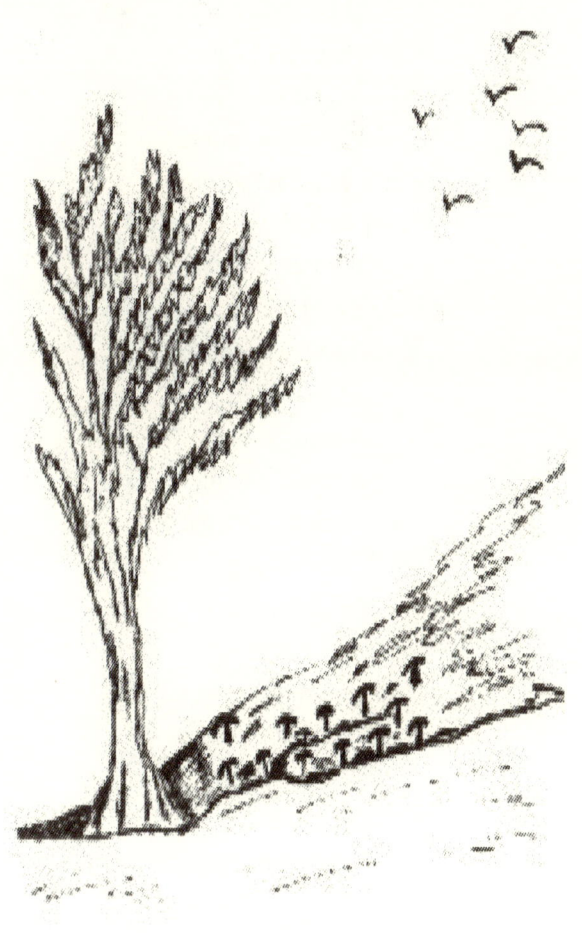

IDIOTIC JUDGE

Who out there
Is a judge-
Why should you
Judge me anyway?

11

What crimes have
I committed
What evil I have
I done.
Why am I standing
In a criminal's court
When I walk down the street
Or enter a mall?
Aren't you appalled
That I, a decent
Human Being
Is being judged
Without having
Committed a crime?
Think about it.
You out there in
The vast universe
Who would judge another
Because of the color
Of his skin.
Who out there
Is a judge?
Why should you
Judge me anyway?
I've done no crime.
I'm innocent and you
Can't find me guilty
In the courts of Divine Justice.

FOUND GUILTY

Guilty! Your Honor, Guilty!
This man is guilty
He was tried before
He was born
He was doomed before
He arrived here.
He shall be punished,
Segregated, sequestered,
Excluded and exhibited
As a reject, and a rogue.
Here comes the Judge
With eyes piercing like a sword,
Clear as flowing crystal waters
Pure as the snowy drops
From heaven above.
What evil has this accused done.
Why is he guilty?
What crime has he committed?
Why is he questioned?
Hush! Hush! Hush! Hush!
No voice is heard
No one speaks
Silence reigns supreme.
Speak up! You who have brought
This man here.
Guilty Your Honor, Guilty Your Honor.
He's guilty, but he has done
No wrong.

Why have you brought him here?
He is guilty
He is guilty
Because he is black.
Guilty, Guilty, when
Will he be tried
And found innocent.

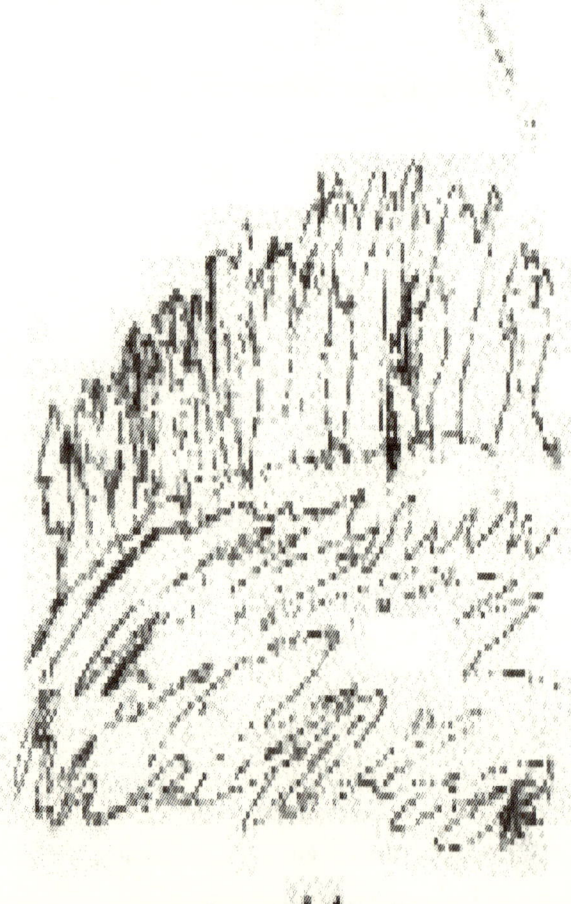

WHAT SHALL I SAY
TO MY CHILDREN

What shall I say to my children?
Should I tell them that there's no hope,
No sparkle that shall burst
Upon their path because they're black?
What is a Black mother to do
To her offsprings
Nestled in her bosom
Or treading life's pathway.
Shall I tell them
Before you tell them
Or should I let them
Find out by themselves
How cold and callous
Is the slice of life.
When shall my children
Discover that they are black.

AMERICA, YOU CANNOT DIE

America, you cannot die
You must live.
You can't be like
Ancient kingdoms recorded
In our history books.
America, America, arise
You must live

17

You cannot die.
Internal decay
Greed, immorality and shame
Have slaughtered civilizations
Of long ago.
America, America arise
You must live
You cannot die.
Your inhumanity to man,
The innocent blood
That was shed
All come to haunt
And to mesmerize;
But repentance
Will heal our wounds.
America, America repent
And begin anew
To bring new life to our shores.
The curse of the slain
Are on our plains
And souls returning
Have come to haunt.
They come in disguise
Yet we see them
Men clothed in women's bodies
Women clothed in men's bodies.
And should I teach them
That they have to pay
For a debt they did not make -
About this great land, America.

Is this a land of the Brave?
How then shall I teach them
To be a coward?
Is this the Land of Liberty?
Then how shall I teach my children
Boundary, subjugation and fear?
Is this the Land of Freedom?
How shall I tell my children
To limit their dreams
And not to scale the mountains
Of adventure and the future?
I'm a black mother
Who wants everything wholesome for my children.
I must teach my children
Courage, strength, fortitude
Determination, and pride.
I must teach my children
Yes, this is America - A
Land of Freedom, Liberty and
Justice for all.
My children are born Americans
And they shall feel no less
Than any American.
So let my children rise to honor
They are proud of who they are
They are proud to be Americans.
Children abused by their own families
Violence, tearing up and down
The Land like savagery.
America, America, you cannot die

You must live

You must live

Stop, Return to Truth and Justice

You must live

You cannot die.

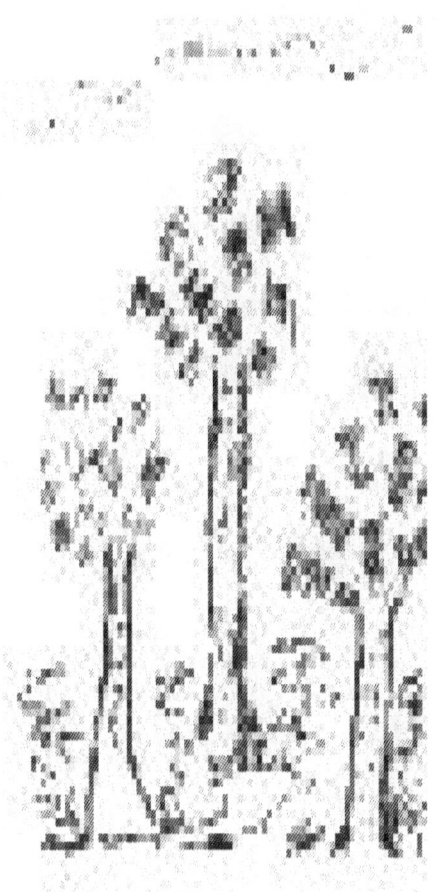

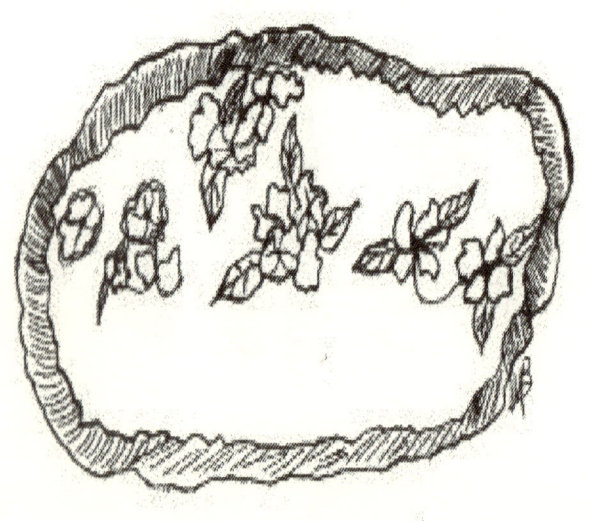

MY BLOOD YOU'LL TRIGGER

Don't call me nigger
My blood you'll trigger,
I'm a proud Black
Star of the night.
Deep within my mortal soul
I have divine light
That makes me
Royalty.
Don't call me nigger
My blood you'll trigger.
That's a bad word
That pierces as a knife.
Don't call me nigger
You're a killer
If that brutish word
Darts out of your mouth.
I'm a black pearl
And that makes me precious.

I AM SOMEBODY

I learned I was somebody
Before you told me
I was nobody
So I don't believe you
No matter what you say.
No matter where you're from,
I know you're a ham
I know who I am.

24

My daddy and mommy
Told me who I am
And that's no sham.
I am somebody
Destined for life
Destined to make
A change in this universe;
So let me tell you in verse
Wherever you are
Whoever you are
Don't judge a man
By the color of his skin
You don't know his kin,
And you may sadly have to admit
You are a fool
Who is not well schooled
To judge others
Before you even know them.
The reality of life is
Color is but a garment
That's the only comment.
Who a person is, is demonstrated
And "niggers" come in all colors.

I'M DIFFERENT

I don't have to be
What you see in me
I am the destiny of my fate
So you are awfully late
To call me nigger
And hope to trigger
Hate, hopelessness and fear
Within my symphonic heart.
I'm a singer of life
I'm a liver of life
The sky is my limit
I'm heaven bound.
You'll never tear me down;
I'm a divine dreamer
Life is MY adventure
And your lame words
Will never keep me down.
I don't have to be
What you think you see in me.
I am the destiny of my life
I am the maker of my dreams
I am the creator of my fate.
I have God walking with me
And I'm walking to conquer.

NO NIGGER

I'm no nigger, brother
I'm a soul sister
Clothed in brown skin
Related to humanity
No matter what your color.
I don't need to devour
Your pride, dignity or dreams

28

I'm a soul sister
Who calls every man brother
And every woman sister.
Life is too sweet
To disrespect people I meet.
Each person is a creation
Of God my heavenly Father
Thus, I rise to bless everyone.
I love everyone whether
Black or white, rich or poor
Even the homeless, I adore
For they too were created by God.
Whatever path they took that led
Them to disaster is not my business
I'll not judge or defame.
I'm a soul sister who loves all
And that's what makes me great.
It's too late to hate
And hate is a disease
I've never had.

QUESTIONS

How can you be
A man of the Law
A man of the Cloth
A man with Integrity
Justice, and Freedom
And call me nigger?
This word indicates that
You've prejudged me

Not letting me be
The person I want to be.
Before you can see
What I'm telling you
Your heart and mind
Have to be purged
From prejudiced hate
And deceit.
Don't call me nigger
Don't stoop lower
Than the word you call me.
Your words shall condemn thee
Thy heart betray thee.
Don't call me nigger
For if that's what you believe
You'll never treat me like a brother.
Cool, callous, calamitous indecency
Stacked like dead men's bones
In the mentality of incivility.
A word can bite like hell
The ringing blast as a tolling bell.
Don't call me "nigger"
I'm a Black Queen
Whether I'm crowned or not.
I'm a queen because I live
Like one and act like one.

ACCOUNTABILITY

Shall we be judged
By the things we say
And the things we do?
Is there a day of accountability
A day when we shall
Be judged in the Courts of Heaven?
Then if this could ever be
Don't speak lightly of me;
Don't call me what I'm not.
Don't look upon my face
And dare to efface
My human race.
So what if you don't
Believe in the Living God;
Possibly that's why
You say the things you say
And do the things, you do.
But believe me, you're accountable
So don't call me nigger,
I'm not your scapegoat
Beating bag or Tarring post.
No one can get away anymore
Now there's an open door
We may all walk in and
Live together in peace
Or rot in separate graves.
You need me and I need you

Don't call me nigger
And cause my blood to trigger.
My inventions have civilized
Your world
My inventions have cured
Your world
My inventions have caused
You to twirl
Above the heads of your competitors.
Don't call me nigger
You need me
And I need you
So respect me
And I know, I'll respect you.

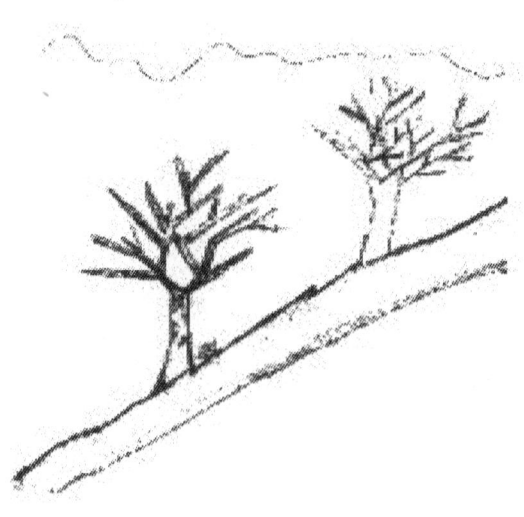

34

YOU DON'T KNOW ME

Tell me what's my name
Tell me who I am
And I'll know you
Even though I don't know you.
Run your mouth
Like an unstopped faucet
And your life's set
Like a molten jello
Shaking and going nowhere.
Anyone who prejudges another
Is not very bright
Because in these days of
Enlightenment
We all should know better.
How can you tell me
What's my name
And you don't know me?
The only way you can
Is if you've prejudged me -
Of course you're completely wrong.
No one can sing my song
Without knowing my melody.
So sing your song
and let's get along
Because there's a tune
For everyone.

STOP NAME CALLING

You've called me
So much out of my name
That even my brothers
And sisters dare to say the same.
Don't call me nigger
Nigger is not my name
Your poignant word
Has pierced the simple minds

Of those who believed
And accepted your defame.
If I stooped to be
What you called me
How damned would be my fate.
But I have to rise
To rise above whatever
Is thought of me.
I know my name
My spirit within me
Rises and soars above
The infernos of lies
Degradation and blasphemy.
I'm a child of God-
Off of me take your hold
I'm free to sing
Like the mockingbird.
My ideologies and philosophies
Take me higher than
Your deceptive word
Could ever soar.
I'm no nigger
I'm Ebony sculptured
By the Omnipotent God.

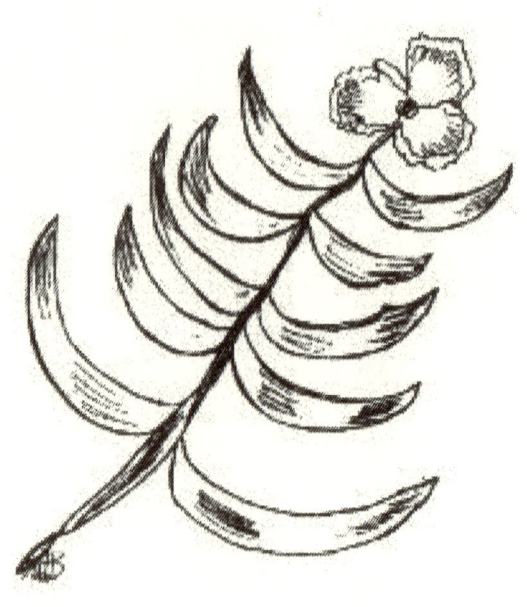

BLACK AND PROUD

I'm Black
And I'm proud
I'm no nigger.
You call me
Names and cause
My blood to boil
And then sit back
In your easy chair
And dare to jeer.
Your mind is an

entanglement of serpents
Lashing out to kill
And to destroy me
But tell me, tell you
I am free
As free as the bird.
Yes, it's no use
To beat and abuse
And then wonder
Why some brothers
Are as wild as
Untamed brutes - killing
Stealing, raping, running.
You made them niggers,
But don't call me
A nigger because I'm black
I'm no nigger
I'm ebony and strong
I've done no wrong
So this is my song
Free at last Free at last
Thank God Almighty
I'm free to be me.

RUNNING OUT

There is a point
Where even angels
Turn to revolt,
And patience
Disappear like the
Morning mist
Before the rising sun;

The Blistering, Burning heat
Of life turns to sonic beat,
And tempers marching
Like million soldiers
Fighting In Desert Storm,
Resist to conquer
Tyrannical enemies
That persist to conjure
Hate, fate and mistake.
It's no time
To call me nigger.
The twentieth century
Is at its close
And minds should
Be free from slavery's curse.
A blast to victory
I hear deep into
My mortal soul.
Don't call me nigger
Or else you may feel my temper
Swelling up like volcanic lava
Then crushed shall be
Thy wretched soul
And hell shall be thy doom.
Don't call me nigger
Unless you want
Your lips to be set on fire
To cool my desire.

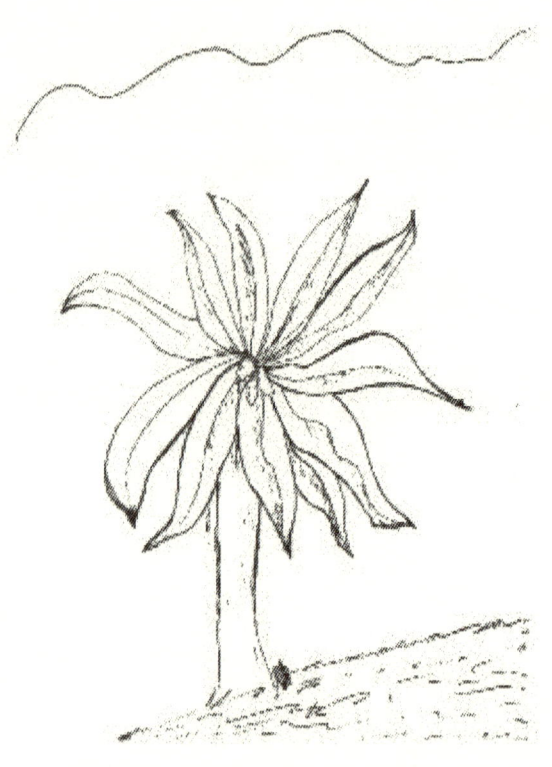

SLAVES IN EVERY COLOR

Slaves have been
In every land
Slaves have been
White, Black
Brown and Yellow;
Yet only one class
Of slaves have
Been called niggers.

Why oh why is this
Declarational curse?
Why oh why is this
Group of slaves degraded?
I'm no nigger because
I was brought to
This United States.
Let the word die
Let the word die
Let the word "nigger," die.
I am ashamed
To be called a "nigger"
The connotation is derogatory
Deflamatory and implicative.
I can't be blamed
For the unmerciful deeds
Of human beings
And to be really correct
Those who took my
Forefathers into slavery
They are truly the niggers.
I'm the victim of social genocide
I've been victimized
And mesmerized
So don't you dare call me, nigger.

CALM

Soft breezes blow
And I'm as calm
As the newborn baby
Who has been fed,
Cleaned and restful.
Nothing alarms me

44

I am as free as the breeze
Blowing through the streets
Of time, not disturbing
The nests of wasps
That swarm around me.
I look at the world
Very optimistically and pray
For peace and love to abound.
I extend my arms
To all who want to find
A place to rest -
That's the very best
That I can do
Because I owe a due
To pay back to life
What I've discovered.
Yet oft times there
Comes a flash out of hell
That stirs my tranquillity
To erupt into a nightmare
Of anger, fury and rage.
Don't call me nigger
You'll explode my world of paradise
Into a battlefield of missiles.
Hold your breath, swallow your words
Purge your mind with the Golden Rule.

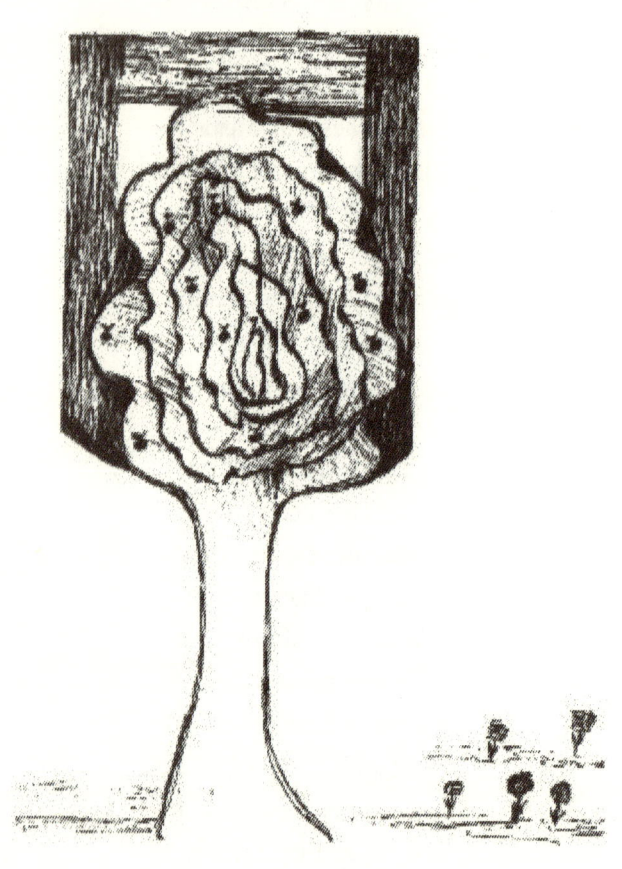

DISTORTED REFLECTION

Claw my heart
Pierce my flesh
Dismantle my dreams
Play massacre with

46

My children born
And unborn -
Call me nigger
And you've destroyed
All I've hoped for,
All my people
Have worked for.
A name is more
Than a name
It tells me what you are
And what I am
In your mind.
Yet, there's no way
I am what you say
Because I know myself
Better than you
Know me.
I shall rise to lofty
Mountains
Where only the greatest
Will achieve.
I'm on my way to leave
To my posterity
A world of freedom, love
And optimism.

I'M PROUD

Don't call me nigger
I was born
In a family I
Did not choose,
But if I lived
A million years
And had my choice

I would not
Choose another.
I'm proud to be black
There were things I lacked
But integrity, fairness
And godliness
Were not the virtues
I miserably missed.
I learned morality
And justice long
Before I even understood
Fully to explain
Why I did the things I did.
I just knew that it was right
To be good
And right to respect myself
And others.
Golden inheritances that mere
Color did not invest in me -
It was my godly father and mother
Who gave me my foundation.
My parents told me who I was
I was the apple of their eyes
Their pride and joy
And today I still hear their melodies,
So don't call me nigger.

I KNOW ME

A great big world of
Ideologies, philosophies
Peoples, countries
All like a boiling pot
Melt in a lava so hot
that could blow one's mind
Completely out of control.

I'm just a speck
In the arena of time
But life has a purpose
For all of us.
There I stand
Unequivocally determined
To give to life
The reason for being.
I really don't have to teach
Nor do I have to preach,
My very presence
Effuse the goodness
And wholesomeness of life.
I smile and broken hearts are mended
I pray and lives are transformed
I touch a face with my kindness
And tears of joy bubble into
Springs of living water.
Don't call me nigger
For I shall laugh you to scorn
I shall laugh in your face
And you'll stand there dumb like a mule
Still like a rotten corpse
Startled like a scared cat
And bewildered like a rat.
I am who I am
And I am proud.

THE TIDE WILL RISE

Waves dashing upon the shores
Keep rolling eternally.
People laughing, talking, playing
Enjoying the goodness of nature
Without paying a dime.
As we're dashed
Upon the shores of time
We should bless all those
Whom we meet.

Laugh a while, smile a while
Sing and dance
To the magical tune
That whistles in the breeze of time.
Soon the tide will rise
And we shall all be taken out
Into Eternity.
Cast hate, prejudice, bigotry
From our doors
And the waves will certainly
Wash them from our shores.
Life's paradise is respecting ourselves
And others
Helping to make the world
A better place
For those who are here
And those who
Will yet follow the universal tide.
So let our words
Be seasoned with grace
Let's love each others race
Then and only then we'll embrace
The true spirit of Brotherhood.

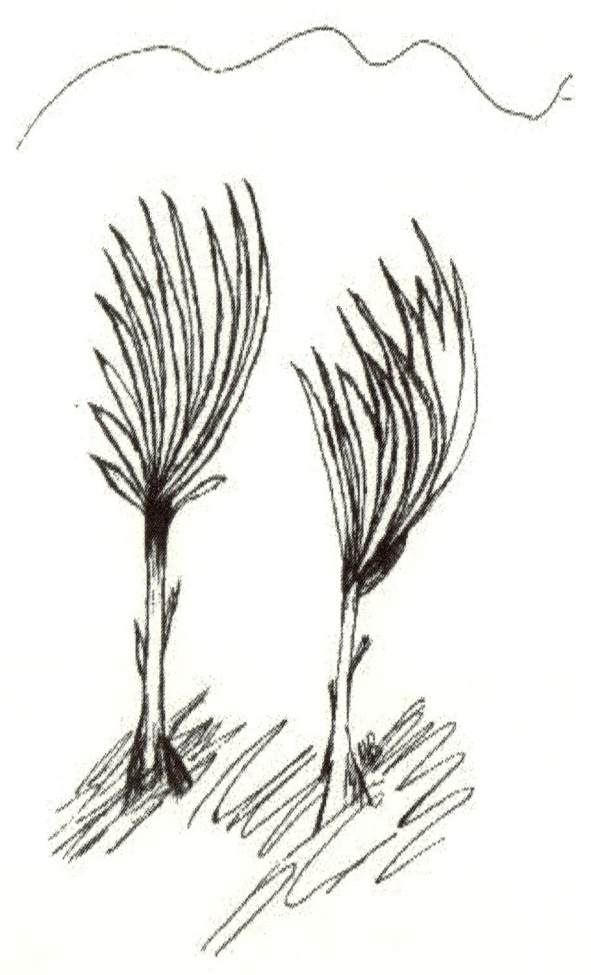

I'M JUST A WAVE

I'm just a wave
Dashing upon the
Shores of time.
How ridiculous to even think
That I'm someone special
While others are not.
Who has made me judge?
What price did I pay
To come to earth
Clothed in whatever flesh
I have found myself?
What ignorant madness
Of inhuman unkindness
To bless my race and curse yours.
Nothing but presumptuous
Horrendous pride could cause
Hearts so blinded by folly.
Don't call me nigger
And stand out there like something special.
Your senseless madness
Will one day prove your blindness.
Death, hell and the grave will
Swallow your fiendish pride.
Somehow I trust before you hit the dust
Illumination will evoke repentance
And your ending will be sweet.

A TINY DROP

I hear the whistling of the waves
The dashing, bursting and lashing
Of the waves as they dash upon the shores.
A tiny drop of water gathered together
To make a mighty ocean.
Each human is a tiny drop
Joining the masses across the lands.
Some are whistling some are laughing
But all are contributing
Whether good or bad
Whether blessings or cursing,
I hear the whistling of the waves
The dashing, bursting and blasting
Of the waves as they dash upon the shores.
Don't call me nigger
You are only a drop of water
In the majestic ocean of time.
You will one day break
Upon the shore
And life will be no more.

SURE TO WIN

I'm warm, tender, loving.
A lump of brown sugar
That's what I am.
I see the world
As God's Creation
Ticking time away
Into eternity.
I'm here for a season
Exploring the reason
Why I'm here, there and everywhere.
And Life is magical
Dramatic and challenging
But the race we're running
We're sure to win
If we trust in the Almighty
Have faith in ourselves
And seek to do no man wrong.
I'm stepping on top of the world
I've achieved so many goals;
Life has been a bundle of joy
Even in the midst of storms.
I've learned well how to succeed
And the thrill of success
Tingles in my blood
Like an effervescent stream.
I'm no nigger
I'm a queen

Sitting on top of my throne.

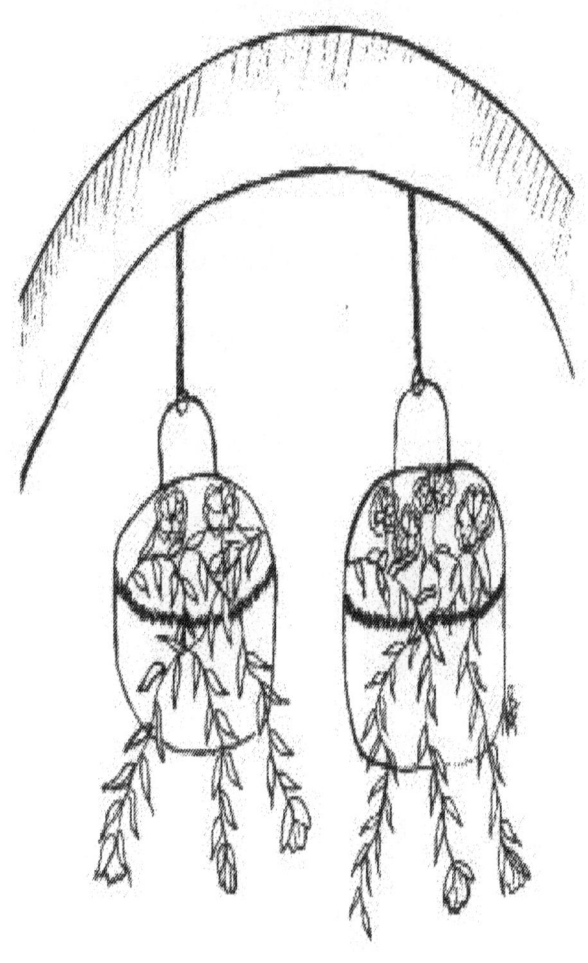

TOUCH MY FACE

Reach your hands out
And touch my face
You'll touch my race
And feel the warm
Throbbing of my flesh.
Touch my eyes
And they will water
Just like any other;
Hear my heartbeat
And you'll begin to feel
The pain within me.

ANGER

My face is like
A raging bull dog
I stand ready for attack
No nonsense is my plea.

I'm a human being,
If you please.
I live my life
I sing my song
I do no wrong
To my fellow
Human Being
Thus, I owe no one an apology.
I simply ask
Don't step into my space
Don't think you can
Run over me
With your cartwheel of injustice
And your hammer of prejudice.
I have to live my life
I have to sing my song
And self preservation
Is the first Law of Nature.
Like a raging bull dog
I stand ready for the attack.
No nonsense is in my face
I'm a part of the Black race
Thus I owe no man an apology.
I simply ask
Don't step into my space
You can't run over me.

MY FACE REFLECTS

Touch my black face
It is warm as the summer's breeze
As golden as the magical hills
In the hot desert lands.
The sun shines into my face
And I feel the heat.

65

I even hear the beat
Of symphonic music
Dancing upon my eardrums.
I look out into the world
And with joy I twirl
I'm free as free
As the wild birds.
I am untamed and reckless.
I fly to the desert lands
And water is scarce
So I drink from the honeysuckle
And the sweetness satisfies me.
I'm prepared to live
And nature surrounds me with blessings.
I sing and I dance in the
Midst of life's madness
Because I'm strong, creative
Industrious, undaunted and fearless;
I'm surviving in the jungles of life
Nobody feeds me with a silver spoon
I'm making it with faith
Determination, perseverance and love.
Yes, love's the magical word
That flashes luminous brilliance
In my darkened pathway.
I'm always moving in the right direction
And my future is bright.
Touch my black face
I'm no nigger.

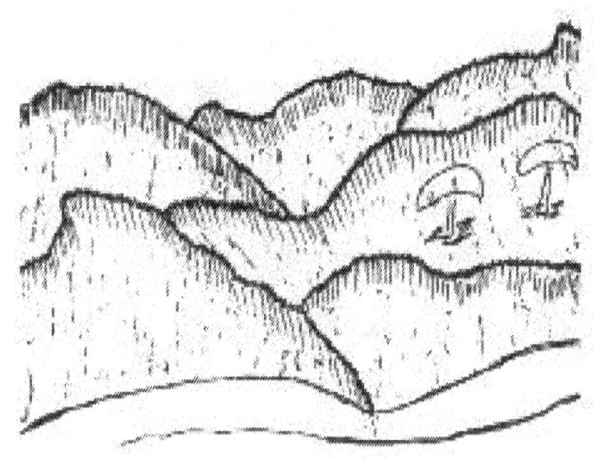

TRANSFORMATION

As I begin to climb
Up into the bosom of the
Mountains leading from

67

Tehachapi to San Luis Obispo
I begin to feel the glorious freedom
Of an exalted awareness of Divinity.
Somehow I am transformed
Into one with nature - not in
A pantheistic sense but
In a divine sense which
Is greater than the realm of the mind.
The spiritual awareness of God
Frees my mortal soul and I
Begin to feel my awareness
As a child of Divinity, a child
Created by an awesome unseen person.
He cradles me in His stupendous hand
And I rise above the dreadfulness
Of life.
I know without anyone telling me -
I'm no nigger.
I'm boundless, I'm free, I'm Body
Soul and Spirit and although
People may destroy my flesh
With brutish lashes and pain
They can't touch my soul and spirit.
Thus I rise! I rise! I rise!
I just keep on stepping
Every obstacle becomes a stepping stone.
Rising, Rising above the clouds
There'll never be any doubts.

SOAR LIKE AN EAGLE

Up from the dust
Of bigotry
Hate and fear
I shall soar
Like an eagle

In the skies.
My thoughts are lifted
To praise and glory
And though I often cry
As I see the
Lashes of injustice
Slap my brothers' faces
I bow in silent prayer
And know there's love
That watches over us.
Somehow we shall be free
To think, to be, to endure
There's an unseen eye
Watching over all.
I'm no nigger
You're no nigger.
We're all God's children
Decked with multiplicity
Of colors.
Like the mighty rainbow
We promise there'll be
A brighter tomorrow -
Up from the dust we shall rise.

I MUST BE FREE

Look in my eyes
Can't you see the pain
Anguish and distress?
Would I be such a mess
If you had treated me right?
Look to the corners of the world

See how flourishing are my brothers.
Yes, they may not have
Material belongings
But my black brothers abroad are proud.
They are brave
They have dignity
They survive better than I do
In this vast united land.
Why, why is this my friend?
They've killed my spirit
Taken my dignity
Stripped me of my heritage
Here I stand naked, raped
And Confused.
But, I'm no nigger
On my knees I bow
Asking the Almighty God to show me
The way to my freedom.
Yes, my body may be free
But Lord have mercy on my soul
My Spirit and soul are bound.
I'm locked in a prison
The chains hold me fast
I must be free at last.
Speak to me blowing free wind
Speak to me flying free bird
Speak to me rolling free seas.
I must be free.

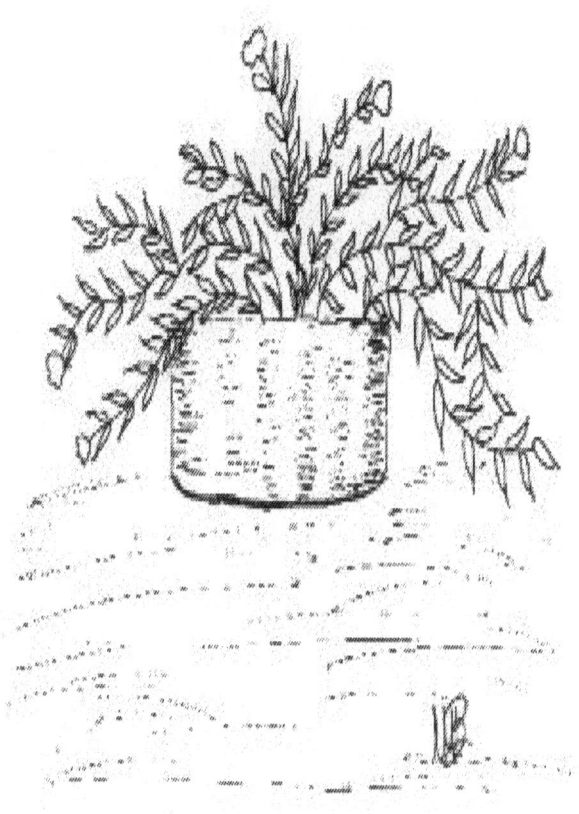

WHO AM I

I'm a child of the Living God
In His omnipotent presence
I rise to my full potentialities.
Biting, blistering, bombastic words
Shall die like flies which have
Been sprayed with pesticide.
I'm in my wonderful world
Dirty names won't hinder me.
Sound, sound your trumpets
Let them blast through time
Until every ear is filled
With triumphant melody.
Let every woman, man boy
And girl hear this symphony of
Sweet, sweet music.
I'm no nigger
I'm Mr. So and So,
Mrs. So and So,
Miss So and So,
Brother So and So,
Sister So and So,
Doctor So and So,
Attorney So and So,
But don't you dare
Call me nigger!
I have a name.

I'M NOT PLEASED

I'm a mad dog
Growling with anger.
Your names have been a curse
Taunting my soul.
Like a million serpents
Stinging me perpetually.

My anger rolls up
Inside of me
Lashes out with turbulence
Violence and crimes.
Angry, astonished, argumentative
I stand at life's
Crossroads
And howl for help
But nobody hears
ME.
They laugh and play
Upon my soul
And wonder why
I'm out of control.
My world was created
By devious people;
I'm a product of their
Machinery
That's why they call me
Nigger
But I'm no nigger.
I'll take off my mask
If you believe in
ME
When I'm free to be
ME
You'll really be surprised
I'll be just like you.
I will be brand new.

LET ME BE FREE

Take the chains
From my mind
Let me believe
In myself;
Let me ride
The tide
Of life freely.
Then and only
Then
You can judge
Me
When I'm free.

REVELATION

Suddenly my night
Turns to day
I believe in
Myself
I set goals for
Myself
And feel the
Calm gust
Of adventure.
I begin to live
Life.

WHO HEARS ME

I'm waving my arms
My back is bleeding
From the lashes of life.
The daggers are in my heart
And blood drops are

Squirting everywhere.
My tears are flowing
So profusely
Drop by drop, drop by drop
They can't stop.
Nobody sees this
Despicable sight of humanity.
Conceited hypocrites from the
Religious, political and philosophical
Hierarchies pass me by daily.
They are too concerned with materialism
Piety and whether or not
Animals are mistreated -
No ill will to our poor animals
At the brutish hands of men;
They too should be considered
But what about me.
But while my terrified portrayal
Of dignity illuminates
The darkness of life
Nobody hears or sees me
For in the pit of my darkness
My mind has lost the sensitivity
Of life
Thus I have become a vicious brut
Killing, robbing, running, hurting.
Society has been my whipping post
As I bleed and hurt not wanting to be
The dehumanized wretch
I've been let to become.

"Nigger," "Nigger," "Nigger." tormented
I sit in my melancholy valley
and pray for change that would
Bring healing to my bleeding heart
Peace to my confused mind
Freedom to my chained spirit
And a chance to transform me.

I'M FREE

Let tigers eat of my flesh
Let them take bread from
My starving mouth
And meat from my children's table.
Let them try to strip
Me of all my dignity,
I shall rise from the tomb
Of life.
I shall not be the brut
People intend me to be
I'm free in my spirit
I'm reigning in my kingdom
I'm lord of my domain
I'm going to be free
No matter where I be
I shall rise to the heights
Of success.
I shall reveal to the world
Who I am
I am a decent citizen of
Any land.

BORN FREE

Liberty and Justice
For all
That's the clarion call
To you
To me

Everyone.
We all have inalienable
Rights
As expressed in our
American Constitution
Thus, I stand a free man -
Innocent
Until proven guilty.
I soar to become my dream
Life is my paradise
I dance to my
Music.
I climb to the stars
And disregard stares
As I soar to my own
Resurrection.
I am no victim
I am a victor
Breaking loose from my cocoon
To become a gorgeous butterfly.
My beautiful world is synchronized
By the melody of my own fingers
For I was born free and shall
Die a free soul.

BLACK AND GUILTY

What is justice?
Am I innocent
Until proven guilty.
Then why am I guilty
Before my case
Is presented in
The Court of Law.
Am I guilty because of
The color of my skin?
Do I have to prove I'm innocent
Because I'm black?
Don't judge me in ways
That you don't judge every
Other man.

MAD JUDGE

Who has the divine right
To give me freedom
Or to take it away?
Who stands as judge
To judge me
When I've committed
No crime?
I stand breast to breast
With every man
My life is not dependent
On you.
My life is in the palm
Of my hands.
I shall reach the Promised Land
Plotted out by Divine hands.

OPTIMISM

I'm effervescing with life.
My blood is warm
Running in my veins
Energizing me to reach
Every star
That is afar.
I'm moving on life's
Parade
I'm not afraid
My pilot leads the way
Each and every day.
I'm destined by Divinity
I'm schooled with dignity
I'm liberated by the fibers
In my own soul.
I'm not curtailed by another's
Whim.
I'm lord of myself
And will stretch my
Soul, my mind to
Their own limits.
Thus, I blame no one for
The scope of my destiny.

IN CHARGE

I'm king
I'm queen.
Society is my
Kingdom.
I usually stretch
Myself
To optimal achievements.
I am in charge of me.

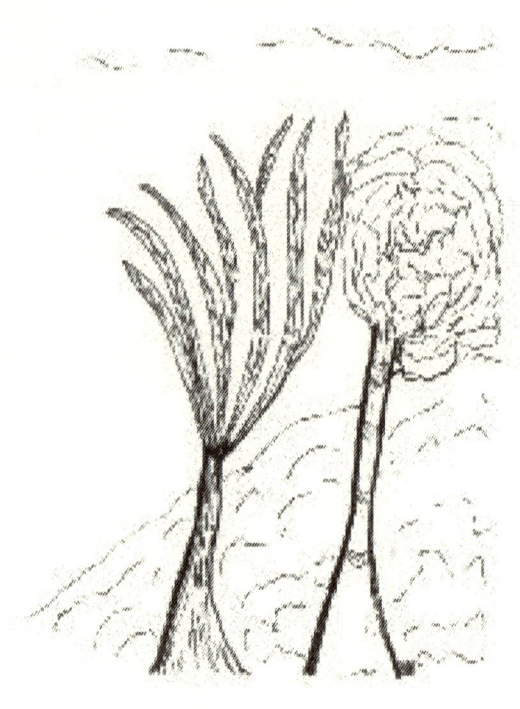

FIREWORKS

Look into my eyes
And see the sparks
Firing like fireworks
Blasting deep into the night.
I'm sick and tired
Of the injustices dished
Out to people simply
On the basis of color.

Am I guilty
Before I have committed
A crime.
Am I guilty because
My color is black?
What awful destination
Of misery and hell.
The inferno burns
With fiery heat
As my heart beats
Like a tom-tom drum
Sending messages across
The distant skies.
Look into my eyes
And see the sparks
Blasting like fireworks
Going deep into the night.
Let prejudice die
Like flies in every state,
In every land.
Justice, freedom, liberty
Respect, dignity of humanity
That's what I ask
That is my prayer.

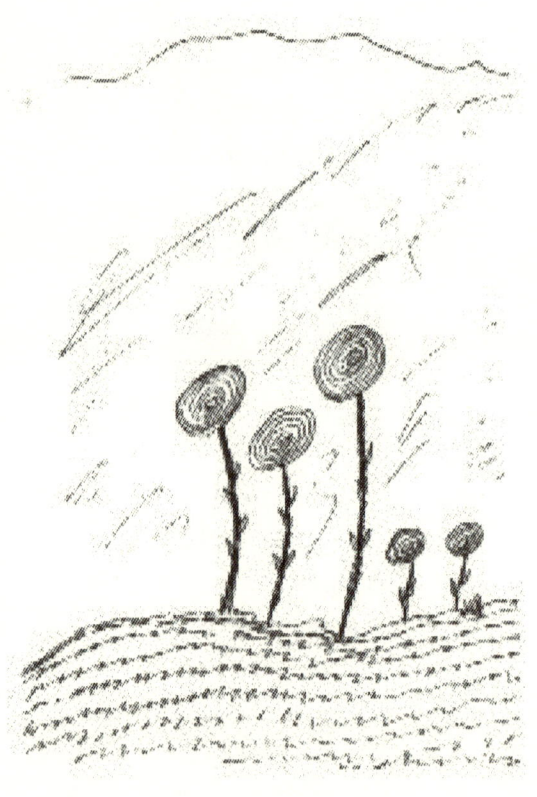

CONTEMPLATION

In an open prison I walk
In a land of liberty
And though I'm free
As free can be
I cannot help but see

Injustice wheeling o'er my head
And wonder if the fears I dread
Will some day find me dead.

UNHOLY SOUNDS

How can I step in life
Laughing with rapturous glee
Clapping my hands and singing
My song
Like I can't hear the crying
Of my brothers and sisters who have
Done no wrong.
Black from across the seas
Where life was filled with glee
But in the heart of a calamitous
Puzzling unpredictable climate
I rise to face the rising sun.
I run my race with sweet embrace
But deep within my imprisoned soul
I'm dazed with unanswered questions.
Plagued by dismal visions of injustice
Don't say the word nigger
He is my brother
His skin looks like mine,
And the word chills my mind
Blowing me out of control
Sending waves of anger through
My spine.
Like an eagle I rise every day
To display to the world the dignity
Of who I am and who you are.
I am my brother's keeper.

HIDDEN PAIN

I walk in dignity
Through the tunnel of life
Sometimes only darkness
Wraps around me
Like a dark dismal cloud.
Nobody knows my name
We all look the same;
Sometimes I seem invisible
As I walk the streets of misery,
Yet courage keeps me stepping.
Nobody sent for me
I came to a land
They told me was free
But found my puzzled mind
Keep ticking as a clock.
Inwardly I've cried my tears
Because of secluded fears.
Have I found the jewels
I came to discover
Or is the price too much
To ease my troubled mind?

LOOK AHEAD

Look ahead,
Look ahead
See the light
In the night
Justice, Liberty
For all
Let the flag
Of liberty flow.
She holds the torch
To foreign souls
Looking with anticipation
Hope and Dreams.
Though I bow
My sacred head
Land of Liberty
Waves with pride.
Though the nights
Have been long
I've never lost my song.
Optimism, pride
And joy
Keep me heading
For the light.
Untold dreams become
Real.
Honors we can all achieve
If thy soul within

Thee
Burns with fire that is bright.
For no one can put out thy light
Ignited by the Living God.

THE RISING SUN

I am the rising sun
That has traveled across
The horizon of time.
I've blazed through space
Achieved hidden dreams
Flowing like the mighty seas;
I am the rising sun.
I am the invisible soul
I've run my race
Determined and undaunted
And because I had faith
In myself
And faith in Divinity
I've climbed unreachable
Mountains
And scaled amazing heights.
Yes, it's not what others
Think of me,
It's what I know about me
That keeps me living
Among the stars
And not clinging to the dust.

I RISE

I rise
Each day
To face
The morning
The evening
The night.
Day is
Here
Day is
Everywhere.
I rise
To see
The glory
Blossoming
In Me
Each and
Every day.
I bow
I thank
I praise
God For what
He has
Done for me.

MY HANDS

I reach my hands
Out to the universe
I open my heart
To the ones
Who blow love petals
To fall upon
My sacred head.
I smell the roses
For so many pose
As true-hearted friends.
They hold my hand
Across the land
And I can feel the pulsation
Of hearts that
really care.
Blessed be the ones who
Plant good seeds
In the breeze
Everyday
For some fall on me
And grow
Deep within my soul.

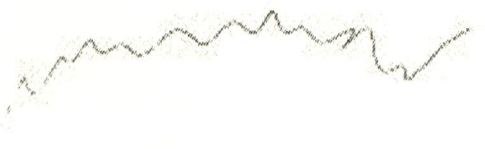

INDIVIDUALS

Everybody
Isn't like
Somebody;
Somebody
Darkened
By
Hate.
Look to the right -
106

Light
Will shine
Through the darkened night.

GOOD PEOPLE

Some people are true
As fresh as the ocean breeze;
They love with love
That is generated by respect
And they create a world
So rejuvenated and bold
That whether black or white
Rich or poor they adore others.
The stand they take is
To give every human soul
A break.
These people stand for
Justice
For Liberty
And Freedom
For
All
They are indeed true Americans -
Land of the free; home of the brave.

HOPE ARISE

I will be
What I want
To be.
Hands are outstretched
Everywhere.
Pessimism, negativism

109

Skepticism and hate
Will blind even the
Eagle's eye.
Life is golden
When hope arises
From the tomb
Of despair.

OUTLOOK

I surround
Myself
With positive
Constructive
People.
I don't have time
For misery.
Love is where
I find it
And I'm color blind
When I
Feel the power
Of love.
Blacks have loved
Me
Whites have loved
Me
Whites have loved
Me
Love itself has no color.

HYPOCRISY

What is this disease
That plagues
My melancholy
Soul
Rolling like ocean billows
Dashing over me -
Duplicity of kindness
And madness
Justice and injustice
Joy and sorrow.
This is a coin
stamped
With heaven and hell
Truth will set us free;
Life is what we make it.
Look to the stars
Keep on stepping
With faith
Everyday.
Taunt your muscles
Paint your face
With a smile
And know when to make
Each move.

WHY

Facing life
Seems maddening
For truth
Seem false
And lies
Appear to be
Truth
The hypocrisy
Of life
Flattens our hope
Scatters our dreams
Makes us wonder
Whether life
Will ever
Be better
For our posterity.
In my cocoon
Life is creating
A magnificent image
Of nature's Miracle
But as I fly
Up in the sky
I can't help
But wonder
Why?

INNER STRENGTH

I pull myself up
From the mire
Of life.
Some bruises I
Caused
Some bruises you
Caused.
Sometimes I did
No wrong
But lashes broke
My back.
My mind mingled
with painful mess
Came to rest
Upon the
breast
Of an invisible friend.
I am never
Alone
As I walk life's streets.
I can make it
I can make it
The rushing strength
Within my soul
Takes me higher than
The stars.

WE ARE ONE

Focus your mind
On the strength
Within you
That's what I
Have done.
Life's battles
Are challenges
For me to build

My muscles
Strong.
Get up from you
ashes
See the shining stars
Looking deeply
Into your soul.
Hear the whistling song birds
Pleasing your ears
With melody.
You can make it
I can too
Nothing is impossible
When we focus
Our minds
Deep within our human souls.
God of our Fathers
Hope of the future
Makes us one.
Out of one blood
He created us
We'll rise to victory
From the battles
Of our land.

I AM STEPPING

I am stepping
On clouds of victory
My dance is motivated
By the force of God
Within me.

I sing my song
I rise to achieve
Every dream I've ever had.
Black as tar
I gaze into the star
And rise to freedom to be me.

I'M IN CONTROL

If I accepted negative words
I would never raise my hands
To build my dreams
On top of the hill.
I would never ever try
I would only sit and cry.
My sorrows would hold me down
Tomorrow,
And my future would be dull.
But negative words ignite
My fire
Set me burning with desire
To make an amazing
Blaze of me
Above the darkened sky.
I fly, I fly
Higher than the dim skies.
I light my fire in the clouds
And dashing through every problem
Comes the illuminating light
That leads us to delight.

TEARS

Silver tears
Roll down
My face.
It hurts me so
To be called

123

A nigger.
You call me names
Your voice
Unheard
But the message
Is clear
The behavior
Is obvious.
Blasting messages
Come to me
Biting my flesh
Piercing my heart
Like hell bursting.
But I regroup
My fainting heart
And rock my soul
Out of control
Of people's miserable
Hell.
I wipe my eyes
Flinch my spirit
Clinch my fist
And knock hell
Out of my way.

I KNOW WHERE TO LOOK

Who pays my bills
Who places food
On my table?
I don't look
To you
To supply my
needs

To make me
happy.
I have the
Power
To rise with
Pride
And get melody
From every note.
I sing my song
I dance for joy
For life's in my
hand,
And your thoughts
Can't hold me down.
Words are powerless
If we dare to confess
I have the power
To take my stand
In this promised land.
So I take my liberty
I take my justice
And give them to all.

WITHIN ME

There is a spirit
Within me
That conquers every
evil

Outside of me.
I am powerful
Beautiful
Sweet.

I'M LOOKING

My eyes flashed
I saw that face
That told me
I was hated.
What did I do
What did I say -
Nothing.
But hate flashed
Like lightning
Out of those
Bloodshot eyes
Like a raging tiger.
The bite was too
Dangerous to
Imagine.
Yet I'm not afraid
I stepped back
Breathed a prayer
And wondered
What madness
Filled the
Wretched heart.

LOVE

When we love
We grow
When we love
We glow.
I have no time

130

To hate a soul.

POWER OF LOVE

None of the evil plots
Shall destroy my dreams
Mightier is the power
Of love
Deep inside of me.
I've passed the test
I've done my best
And the rest
Is up to everyone
Outside of me.
I'm happy within
Life is a magnificent
Paradise.
I smell the flowers
Every single day
Sometimes I pick
A rose
And pass it close by
Peradventure
Its fragrance will
Revive a dead
And wicked soul.

CHAINS BROKEN

I break my chains
I am free.
I am free
To break my chains.
There is a light
That shines within me
There is a higher power
That rests upon me.
Legislate my freedom
If you please,
But I am liberated
By Divinity.
Nonsense word
May curse my race
But I am set free Inside of me.

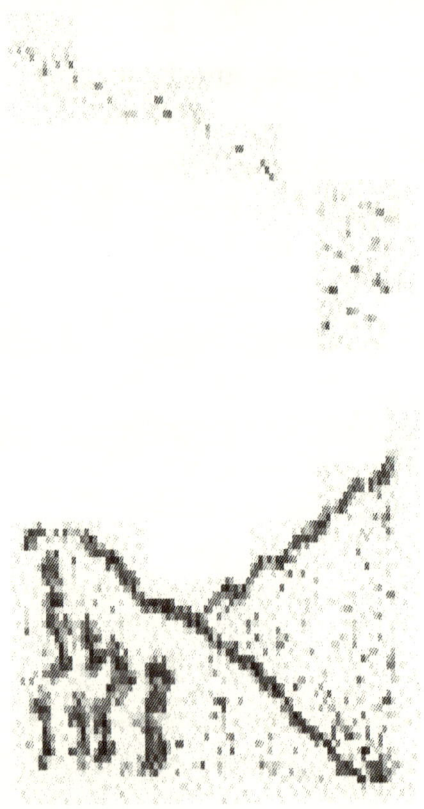

GET UP

Get Up
Get UP
Don't sit
Around
Twiddling

134

Your thumbs
giving in
To doubts.
You can
Do it
You can
Do it.
Believe
In yourself-
Begin Today.

POSSIBILITY

Stretch your hands
To meet mine
Together we will
Make a better world

THRONES

We shall reign
On our own
Thrones
So build with
Gold
Silver
Brass
Precious
Stones
Diamonds
Emeralds
Rubies
And gemstones.
Let every structure
Be girded with
Love
Hope
Peace
And joyful our lives
Will forever be.

BRIGHTER DAY

I'm optimistic
Hopeful
and Prayerful
That life will bloom
Again.
Fear, distrust and hate

Must Dissipate.

TOGETHERNESS

Seeds
Of kindness
Are planted
By every race.
I'm so happy
Love knows
No color.
What a great
World,
When we join
Together
To share inventions
Science and technology;
To make our land
The greatest
Land.
Seeds
Of kindness
Multiply with love.
We shall conquer
Hatred
Through the power
Of love.

RENEWAL

I stretch
My hands
Not for a tip-
I don't need

141

Your pennies.
I simply want
To say
Let's be friends.
The path on earth
Has nurtured
Wars untold.
Let's stretch out
Our hands
To heal all wounded souls.
Let's lift the fallen
Mend the broken,
Repair hopes that are
Torn down.
We can do it, yes we can
Let's decide to start
Today.
Life is short we're not here
For long
Hate will destroy us
Prejudice will blind us;
Let's stretch our hands
To say we are sorry.
Today we shall
Love each other
With a pure and willing
Heart.

DREAM AGAIN

When I would give up
think of the power
that lies within me.
Then I arise to dream
Again

143

Love again
Laugh again
and
Work again.
Life becomes my paradise
I am healed
My broken heart begins to flutter like a bird
I begin to fly.

GET UP

Get up
From the dust.
You're lazy
If you lay
In the gutter
Of your foolish
Heart.
You must believe
In yourself
Trust the future
Work with tenacity
Walk in dignity.
Life will switch
To blessing,
Dust will turn
To gold.
Confess joy and
Happiness
And nothing will be
Impossible.

I CREATE MY WORLD

Whether you call me
Nigger or not
I know who I am.
I make my strides,

Not to meet you
But to move to yonder mountain
Of praise.
I praise my God
For making me
The ruler of my
Domain.
I sing my song
I've done no wrong
And no one shall enslave me.
I move with majesty
I am Royalty.
I climb with praise
Because of gratitude.
How can a clown make a mess
Out of me
When I am free to be
What I want
To be?
If I'm not a king in your kingdom
I am a King
Where I live-
I create my world
With or without you.
It's rough and it's tough
But there's no doubt,
I am in charge
Of me.
I know who I am.

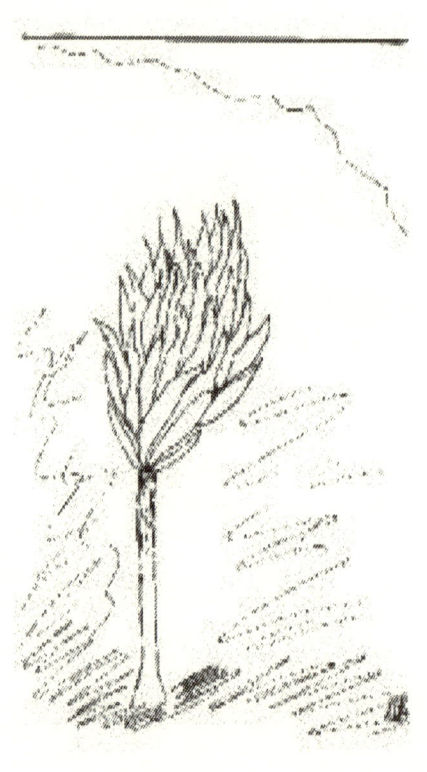

COMFORT

I speak a word of comfort
To every bleeding heart
I see them crying
From various lands afar.

I bow my head in prayer
For every broken heart
It matters not from whence
they come
I love each and every one.

SISTERS AND BROTHERS

My sisters and my brothers
Come in all colors
For they come from every land
East, West, North and South.
I teach their children
For many years
I love them all
Whether Black or White
Red or Brown.
Each soul is pure
As dripping snow
I truly know
God created them all.
So let the tide
Of love
Rise in my soul
I have a job to do
Before I die.
If one person I touched
With my written words
An angel shall arise in
The skies.

A CHANGE

There have been times
When I had to lash out
Like tigers chained in fear.
People were so inconsiderate
That I became quite irate.
But as I demonstrated
Who I was fear melted
Like snowdrops.
Understanding created friendships
That lasted years and years.
Prejudice is a form of ignorance
That locks the minds of people,
But love can unlock the bars
That keep us far apart.
Respect, Respect, Respect my friend
Shall dissipate the curse of hate;
Let's consider the diabolic curse
That separates our hearts.
We need each other to build
Today and tomorrow.
We move to conquer the future
Only by coming respectfully together.
Cries of joy, Cries of joy
To heal every broken life.
Our future shall be brighter
Our children shall be free
To wave our American flag

With pride and dignity.

A BLAST

Look out there!
Thousands are holding
Their fingers deep
Into their ears.
They don't care to listen
To enlightening message.
But if they don't accept
The message today,
They'll understand the blast
Of hate that shall
Erupt like thunder
Across the dreadful skies.
Listen, Listen
Hear a story
Of a painful, hurting
Sobbing heart.
Life will teach us
Peacefully or dreadfully
The simple truths of life -
Human beings are bleeding
Pleading for peace
Listen, Listen before it's
too late.
Time is quickly passing by
Golden opportunities
Will soon be past.
Our civilization craves for peace

In each and every heart.

REALITY

Step out of my space
You're blocking my way
You don't have the right
To hinder me.
You're flesh, I'm flesh
You have to die
I have to die.
You're an ignoramus
To be so ridiculous
To think your color
Makes you king
My flesh will rot
And so will yours
You're not indispensable
So stop your rubbish.
I don't admire your languish -
You know you're blind.
Why not open your eyes
The light will come in
If you are to see.
But as for me
I'll be stepping ahead.

RESULTS OF HATE

Men, women
Boys and girls
Chained and barred
Like wild animals.
Society creates

157

The herd
That howls with
Violence
Magnetized by
Hate
Victimized by
Laws
That violate
The dignity
Of humanity.
I cried in
Shame
But who do I
Blame
When others decide
My wounded fate.
They do their
Work in mess
And shame and
Dare believe that
I am guilty.
What is justice?
What is Truth?
Who is there
To believe me.
I'm guilty before
I'm tried
Lord, have mercy - I'm tired.

TRUTH

Tried by jury
Tried by fury
Give the truth
Whatever the story.
What is it
That justice is
But was the
Truth inside
Of me.
Prosecutors
Defenders
Hear selected facts.
Truth is what
We want to find
Your side
My side
Truth is justice
Truth is blind
Truth knows no color.

MOVE

Don't procrastinate
In front of me
I'll knock your
thoughts
Outside of your
head.
Just move along
And mind your
Own business
For I'll mind my own.

JUDGEMENT

I tremble
At the judgment seat
Lord have mercy
If I am poor.
For if I'm guilty
Before the facts
Are told
How shall I get
My story heard.
Guilty! Guilty!
I am damned
Lord have mercy
On my soul.

WAKE UP

Black man
Rocking his head
Like Samson
In Delilah's lap
Soon he'll be slapped

With inhumane lashes
Upon thy sacred heart.
Judge thyself
Oh heart of clay
Life is a funny game.
Sorrow flashed in
Different ways
So watch your days
As well as nights.
Never forget your race
Remember your face
Is painted with tar.
Act like a man.
Whatever you do
Keep your dignity
With you
Keep your hands
To thyself
Watch as well as
Pray
For one day you'll
Have to find the
Way
To escape.

FAITH

I have faith
In tomorrow
So though
I sorrow
Today
Tomorrow the pain

Will be gone.

I'M MOVING

I'm burning
On fire
With the
Passion of
life.
I'm moving
With ease
To erase
The bitterness of
Life
Time will heal
Every wound.
I pray this
is true
For you and me.
Hurt my brother
And you'll hurt
Me
Whether HE's Black
White
Brown or Red.
No human
Should suffer
Without
A cause.

HOPE

My back is sore
From the burdens
Of life.
My heart feels like a ton
But there is a
Hope
That ignites my flames
To burn and burn
Until all pain
Is gone.
I burn my hate
I bury my fears
I keep on stepping
Ahead
For tomorrow lies ahead
Like paradise
In my head.
What magic of a human
Soul
Creating something from
Nothing
Only Divinity could reveal
The passage from death
To life.
Thus I'm alive to live
In abundance of love and peace.
My pathway is not always easy

But so also is polished gold.
I am a circle of golden
Imagery
My worth is priceless
There's only one of me.

DARKNESS

I feel the blackness
And darkness of night.
Hell is raging in
Every color.
Violence, terror
And fear
Mesmerize society in
Every color.
What a rage
What a disgrace
Man's inhumanity
To man
Has to prove
The equality
Of all.
Violence and crime
Are disguised
Within human hearts.
Oh terror of the midnight
That leads to prayer
For all
Madness raging in every color
Seeking to devour.
We'll have to unite
Or die apart
I feel the blackness
And darkness of the night

Crime is in every color.

A SMILE

A smile
Is a smile
No matter what
The color of the skin.
So smile
And have a
Sunny day
In each and every way.
What blessedness
To smile
Even if you call
Me nigger,
I'll have a sunny day
While your day
Will be mingled
With sorrow.
Words are blows
Of a different sort;
They don't hurt
If we don't permit them.
So I'll smile
My tears away
And sing every day,
For a smile
Washes cares away.
A smile is a smile
That keeps the heart alive.

STEP BACK

Step back!
You're blocking
My way
You're stopping
Progress.
You're holding

172

Yourself back.
Don't stand still
Fighting with me
Keep stepping
Into the future.
You sit on my head
But you can't leave
My bed
As long as you
Lay on top
Of me.
You're squeezing my
Life
Outside of me
But when I am dead
You'll have to bury
Me.
Then you'll be free
To care about
Me.
If you think I'm joking
Just stick around
The odor will be foul
And you'll have to come
See about
ME.

FORGIVENESS

If I didn't forgive
Those who had sinned
Against me,
My sins would
Not be forgiven;

So though horrendous
The crimes
And sinful the shame,
Help me, Oh God
To forgive and forget.
My lack of forgiveness would fester
And corrode
Like cancer within
My mortal soul,
So grant me the strength
To forgive and forget
And look forward to
A brighter day.
I'm singing the songs of forgiveness
I'm singing the songs of freedom
They walk
Hand in Hand together .
Deep in my mortal soul.
Every hurt shall blossom
Into a rose,
Every lash will roll out
Into a golden rod.
Lessons I've learned are
Invaluable
Only sorrow could have
Produced them.
I'm better for every stroke.

THE GOLDEN RULE

Silently I bow my head
Life is swiftly moving ahead;
I live by the Golden Rule
Which I learned in my Home School.
There's no evil that shall devour me
I'm as free as free can be.
Every day I rise to victory
I walk with Divinity
And experience love in my heart.
The tools of righteousness
Shall destroy the bondage of hate,
Silently I bow my head
Life is swiftly moving ahead.
I'm proud to be a star
In the night of life.
I treat others the way
I want to be treated.

A CONQUEROR WITHIN

Though my heart
Sometimes bleeds
And my mind
Twirls like a top,
I can't afford to stop
Living my life
And being me.
I set sail
Out in the ocean of time
The heavy clouds
Descend upon me
Leaving me blind
In a cloud of antics.
Powers rise and fall
But I move ahead
Blasting the barriers
Destroying my foes
That are within me.
I'm not afraid
Of the outside elements,
I'm especially watchful
Of the enemies that are within.
These are the ones
That can destroy me.
I rise to overcome fear
It will cripple me.
I rise to overcome hate

It will cause me to disintegrate.
I rise to overcome procrastination
It will lead me to destruction.
I rise to overcome bigotry
It will lead me to captivity.
And so it is, all negativism
Must be conquered by optimism
As I rise to conquer
As I rise to be the glorious person
I was sent here to be.
I rise, I rise, I rise
And I have joy within me.
I have love within me
I have hope in the palms
Of my hands
I am somebody
I know who I am.

A NEW COVENANT

I want to shout
With a voice loud
And clear
I'm just as good
As you out there.
Tear down the
Barriers
Set me free
And let me be
Who I want to be
I'm nobody's nigger
I never was.
I don't ever
want to be
The shady image
The distorted view
You knew of me.
I'm proud I'm black
I'm moving ahead
I've built cities
I'm a vital part
Of the universe.
Don't blame me if I
Act like a pig
You've given me slop
And created my pen.
Don't blame me for

Being homeless
When I am jobless.
Bread, shelter and food
I have been deprived.
But out there in the dark,
dismal masquerade of life
I shall rise from the rubble
I shall rise from
Despair
And new life shall appear.
Come on my
Brothers and Sisters
Let's move ahead
With faith in
Our hearts
And hope in our breasts.
A new generation
We must create
And our homes
Shall be the kingdoms
Where learning will start.
Let's teach our children
Love and respect
For Self and for others
And our native land.
A new heart
A new spirit
We shall acquire
In order to rise and achieve
Our goals.

NEW IMAGE

I shall rise
From the ashes
Of despair
To walk in the
Newness of life.
I shall know no fear
I shall speak no evil
Life is bursting within me.
I rise to the mountain top
Of glory
And the beauty of my image
Is created by Divinity
No man shall hinder me.
My muscles are fired up with
Divine Energy
I'm destined to create a world
Of mystery and vitality.
No man shall stop me now
I can see a radiant rainbow
Depicting Jehovah's covenant.
I shall take my place in the universe
My children, your children
And our grandchildren
Shall be a new generation
Seeking for life's satisfaction.
We shall not be mesmerized
By shallow dreams that compromise

We're heading for gold.
The journey will not be easy
We'll have to work with tenacity
Pray with fervency
Fight with faith and fortitude,
But we shall see the dawning
Of a New Day.
Every boy, every girl
Of every color, every creed
Shall rise to call this nation blessed.
Desires, Hopes, Dreams shall
Return, and we shall wave
The flag of victory
And feel pride running up
And down our spines.
We are the heritage of this land
Therefore we shall stand.

IT COSTS ME

Burning with sorrows
From life's miseries
I'm one and only one,
But as I touch
Each benighted soul

He rises to face life
With hope.
Thus I touch every soul
That I can reach
And make a difference,
But I pay a price.

THINKING OF OTHERS

Look in my face.
See the lines
Planted by stressful
Years
Moving me to think with
Tears
As I reach out with
Faith
To lift fallen humanity.
What can I say?
What can I do?
Where shall I go?
Open my heart to everyone
Wipe tears from my eyes
Swollen with grief
Smile with joy to transform
Lives in hell.

CAN'T STOP

Stop! Stop reaching out
To others
Stop! Stop trying to
Discover truth -
Voice whispers deep within me

187

Driving me insane.
But blast off
The spark of life
That burns within me,
Keeps speaking in
A voice boisterous
And clear.
I'm motivated, inspired
Driven almost with
Madness
To reach out to others,
Saying a kind word
So life can be changed
And dreams created.
I can't stop
I must keep
Going
Moving
Trusting
Hoping
Caring
Sharing
Knowing
That I am my brother's
Keeper.

MY POSTURE

When I look at you -
Mad as hell,
Something triggers a
Smile
And somehow my anger
Turns
To Love
I feel nothing but peace
Peace perfect Peace.

UNIVERSAL CALL

Wash your minds clean
Of every false
Thought of your brother.
Break the chains of prejudice
Life's madness is
Only rotten dreams
That crash in the realm
Of reality.
Time is out
Finality comes to prejudice
In the hearts of
Blacks
Whites
Brown
Reds
Let's accept each other
With respect and honor
We all need
Freedom.
We all need love.

ABOUT THE AUTHOR

Marjorie Yvette Booker was born in Kingston, Jamaica, West Indies. She received her early education in Jamaica and in London, England. After moving to the U.S.A. in 1954 she later graduated from L.I.F.E. Bible College, California, State University at Los Angeles (B.A.), Pepperdine University (M.S.) and the American International University (Ph.D.).

Dr. Booker has taught in the L.A.U.S.D. for twenty-eight years, and is the founder and President of the Christian Foundation School, Inc. for the past twenty-seven years. She has literally touched the lives of thousands of children and adults during her years of teaching and ministering.

She has received many awards of distinction: Most Admired Woman of the Decade (given by the Board of International Research of the American Biographical Institute); Certificate of Appreciation from the School of Education (University of Southern California). Her autobiographies have been published in Who's Who in California, and Foremost Women of the Twentieth Century, 1988, Cambridge, England.

Most of all, Dr. Booker loves the Lord and is dedicated to do His will